CREATING A SURVIVOR FILE

END-OF-LIFE PLANNING: A SIMPLE FRAMEWORK

CHRIS MEISINGER

Copyright 2023 Chris Meisinger

❦ Created with Vellum

CONTENTS

Chapter 1 — 1
What is a Survivor File?

Chapter 2 — 7
What Items Should be Included?

Chapter 3 — 17
Essentials

Chapter 4 — 21
Assembling the File

Chapter 5 — 27
Important Contacts

Chapter 6 — 29
Funeral and Burial

Chapter 7 — 33
Advance Directives

Chapter 8 — 37
Official Documents

Chapter 9 — 39
Care and Support for Dependents

Chapter 10 — 43
Assets and Valuables

Chapter 11 — 57
Income Sources

Chapter 12 — 61
Accounts

Chapter 13 — 65
Services

Chapter 14 — 69
Bank Accounts

Chapter 15 — 73
Medical Providers and Medical History

Chapter 16 — 77
Health Insurance

Chapter 17 *Life Insurance*	81
Chapter 18 *Long Term Care Insurance*	83
Chapter 19 *Other Insurance*	85
Chapter 20 *Charitable Donations and Philanthropy*	87
Chapter 21 *Small Businesses*	91
Chapter 22 *Personal Messages*	95
Chapter 23 *Show How Much You Care Even After You're Gone*	97

1

WHAT IS A SURVIVOR FILE?

Unfortunately, it is not uncommon for a family dealing with their grief and sorrow at losing a loved one to take on the additional burden of trying to make sense of the financial and material details of their loved one's life. And given the time-sensitive nature of some of the decisions needed, the difficulty is compounded by urgency.

Ask anyone you know who has been responsible for wrapping up the affairs of a loved one, and they will likely express frustration at the amount of time and effort it took to make sense of their personal records.

Many of us assume that our situation is different. We're very organized, our finances and business relationships are well documented, and we can find what we need when we need it. That may be true, but making sense of someone else's organizational system is very rarely easy.

Then, of course, there are others of us who are very aware that they do *not* have a good organizational system. For them, they'll also personally benefit from the process of developing a Survivor File.

The purpose of this book is simple: to provide a few simple steps for you to take on the path towards having your records organized for yourself (if they're not already) and organized in such a way that your survivors are relieved of a lot of unnecessary stress, giving you the peace of mind which comes with knowing that you have done what you can to make a difficult time a lot less difficult for those you leave behind.

It is our firm belief that with a reasonable investment of time and effort, anyone can leave an understandable and organized explanation of all the information their survivors will need!

ALREADY HAVE AN ESTATE PLAN OR WILL?

Kudos to you if you are one of the minority who have created an Estate Plan or a Will or both! The importance of these legal documents should not be overshadowed by the need for a Survivor File.

But even with a Will or Estate Plan in place, you still have a little more work to do to ensure your survivors have the information they're going to need. Both of these legal documents have specific purposes, but neither covers all contingencies.

For instance, imagine you work with a legal professional to create your Will, hoping to ensure that your survivors receive all that they are entitled to and that your assets do not get tied up in probate. Well done! But be aware that there are certain assets (such as pension funds and IRAs) that cannot be transferred in a Will. For these, you need to name a beneficiary. If you don't, the funds can get tied up in probate for a long time. And worse, if your survivors don't know about the account (which is where the Survivor File comes in), the funds may sit in the account indefinitely. It is an unfortunate fact that, in pension funds alone, hundreds of millions of dollars currently sit unclaimed across the country. Some of this belonged to people who had wills, but they did not have a Survivor File to make their survivors aware of the existence of their pension fund account.

MORE ON WILLS...

A will, also known as a Last Will and Testament, is a legal document created to provide the person's final wishes and instructions about managing their affairs and distributing their assets after their death. Only about 40% of adults in the United States have wills.

If you anticipate any conflicts or disputes among your survivors concerning how the instructions you give in your Survivor File are carried out, you should consider having an attorney or qualified legal professional (licensed for your jurisdiction) draft a legally binding will, because the legality of instructions you leave in your Survivor File may be contested.

As already mentioned, besides what is contained in a will there are other vital pieces of information that one's survivors will need, and that's the purpose of a Survivor File. If you have a will, it should be included in your File. If you do not, the written instructions you leave in your File take on even greater significance.

For those who do have a will, please note that you may have already addressed some of the information items listed in the following categories in your will. When that is the case, you can direct your survivors' attention to your will for that information.

WHO IS THE SURVIVOR FILE FOR?

When I write my Survivor File, who am I writing for… who's my intended audience?

Great question! The answer could make a big difference in what and how much information you provide. So it is essential to settle this before getting started.

The fact is we can never have 100% certainty on this point because we cannot predict the future.

For those who are married, their spouse may be the most likely audience. But to make that assumption when writing the Survivor File is not a good idea. Better to write for those less-familiar with your personal affairs, just in case it turns out that sometime in the future, neither you nor your spouse are able to manage your affairs.

The old proverb "better safe than sorry" is applicable here. When writing your Survivor File, imagine the audience being someone who has **very little familiarity with your personal affairs**. It will take a little extra effort but could pay huge dividends in the future.

2

WHAT ITEMS SHOULD BE INCLUDED?

The first step in developing a Survivor File is identifying all the items you want to include. Read through the Documentation List below and decide which items you would like to have in your File and which are irrelevant to your situation. You will also likely think of other things you want to include.

Each section of the list will be dealt with in greater detail later in the book, so it is optional to begin gathering the items now. If an item you want to include is not currently available, though, you should start locating and acquiring it now.

DOCUMENTATION LIST

ESSENTIALS

- Your Will
- Your Estate Plan
- Trust documents
- Contact info for the person or firm that helped create your Will, Estate Plan, and/or Trust
- Power of Attorney
- Location of tax records

IMPORTANT CONTACTS

- Financial adviser
- Lawyer
- Accountant
- Tax return preparer
- Insurance broker

FUNERAL AND BURIAL

- Your Instructions
- Cemetery and funeral home pre-arrangements
- Funeral home contact

- Church contact

ADVANCE DIRECTIVES

- Living Will
- Durable Power of Attorney for Healthcare (Health Care Proxy)
- Do-Not-Resuscitate (DNR) / Life support orders
- Palliative care orders

OFFICIAL DOCUMENTS

- Birth certificate
- Marriage license
- Divorce papers
- Birth certificate/adoption papers for minor children
- National ID card
- Passport
- Citizenship or naturalization certificate
- Residency permit or Visa
- Drivers license
- Auto titles
- Social security card
- Academic degrees and transcripts

CARE AND SUPPORT FOR DEPENDENTS

- Minor children: instructions for care, financial support, and guardianship arrangements
- Elderly parents: instructions for care and financial support
- Individuals with special needs: instructions for care, financial support, and guardianship arrangements
- Pets: instructions for care, financial support, and guardianship arrangements

INSURANCE

- Health
- Life
- Umbrella
- Employer death benefits
- Long term care
- Auto
- Homeowner or renter
- ID Theft
- Other

ASSETS

- Property deeds
- Cemetery deeds
- Timeshare ownership
- Notes held (loans by you to others)
- Vehicle titles
- Safe deposit boxes
- Stock certificates
- Brokerage accounts
- Bonds
- Investments – stocks
- Investments – commodities
- Investments – real estate
- Investments – currencies
- Currency (foreign and domestic)
- Partnerships and corporate ownership
- Digital assets
- Intellectual property
- Heirlooms

INCOME

- Employer
- Social Security
- Pension
- Annuities
- IRA distributions

BANKING

- Savings account
- Checking account
- Money Market account
- Certificate of Deposit
- Line of credit

LIABILITIES AND EXPENSES

- Mortgage documents
- Rental or leasing agreements
- Loan documents
- Utilities
- Credit accounts – Visa, American Express, etc.
- Credit accounts – stores, online retailers, etc.
- Memberships and subscriptions
- Online cash sending/receiving services – Paypal, Venmo, Wise, etc.
- Home utilities – electric, gas, trash, cable, internet, phone
- Maintenance contracts (lawn service, pool service, AC service, etc.)
- Highway toll systems (you may have a balance owed or due)

CREATING A SURVIVOR FILE

- Online retailers (with whom you have established an "account" to submit an order —Amazon, Zappos Shoes, etc.
- Amazon paid subscriptions (music, TV channels, etc.)
- Apple paid subscriptions (iCloud, Apple Music, etc.)
- Entertainment (Netflix, YouTube, Hulu, Paramount+, Disney, etc.)
- Online buying & selling (Craigslist, eBay, etc.)
- Prescription delivery services (OptumRX, GoodRX, CVS, etc.)
- Travel services (Airbnb, VRBO, Expedia, Renta-Car, Uber, Lyft, etc.)
- Convenience services (Grubhub, Instacart, etc.)
- Online Services with a monthly or yearly fee (Microsoft Office 365, etc.)
- Online memberships (paid instructional sites, etc.)
- Club memberships (AARP, AAA, etc.)
- Subscriptions (newspapers, magazines, wine clubs, etc.)

CHARITABLE DONATIONS AND PHILANTHROPY

- Instructions regarding charitable donations
- Instructions regarding establishing trusts or foundations

MEDICAL PROVIDERS AND MEDICAL HISTORY

- Primary care
- Specialists
- Dentist
- Optometrist
- Medical history
- Veterinarian for pets

SMALL BUSINESS

- Contact information for professional services
- Resource inventory
- Product inventory
- Suppliers and vendors
- Clients and customers
- Contracts
- Bookkeeping records

- State corporation commission filings
- Official correspondence
- Corporate tax records

PERSONAL MESSAGES

[In written, video, or audio format]

- Personal messages
- Words of wisdom
- A Sense of one's life story
- Expressions of love and appreciation
- Shared memories
- Guidance for the future

3

ESSENTIALS

Since it will likely take some time for your survivors to familiarize themselves with the contents of your File, and there are some essential pieces of information they will probably need almost immediately, it is good practice to include that information at the very front of the File, so they do not need to hunt for it.

- Your Will, Estate Plan, and/or Trust (if applicable)
- Contact info for the person(s) or firm(s) that helped create your Will, Estate Plan, and/or Trust
- Power of Attorney
- Location of tax records
- Home security system (location of panel and the control codes)

- Home WIFI system (location of modem/router; name and password)
- Garage door code
- Entry door codes
- Location of water and gas turn-off valves
- Location of electrical breaker panels
- Location of irrigation controls
- Location of user manuals (appliances, security system, etc.)
- Location of keys (to vehicles, buildings, property, safe deposit boxes, etc.)
- Social Security number
- Drivers license number and expiration date
- Car license plates and VINs
- Phone number (particularly the one associated with your accounts)
- Home address
- Email address
- Employer / address / phone
- If your survivors will benefit from using your personal computer (for instance, with links to your account websites already saved), you should also include these three pieces of information:

1. Which computer is yours, and what is its password? If there is more than one in the household, how will they identify the one which contains your information? When you restart your computer, are

your required to enter a password? (Remember, your survivors cannot use fingerprint or face ID.)

2. What is your phone's password? Survivors may need to view a security code on your phone when attempting to log on to one of your accounts.

3. What is your email address, the email service you use, and the login credentials you use to access the email service website? Again, survivors may need to receive an email with a security code when attempting to log on to one of your accounts.

4

ASSEMBLING THE FILE

Once you have identified the items, the next step is to assemble them into a Survivors File in an organized way, making it easy to understand and use by your survivors.

PHYSICAL (PAPER) DOCUMENTS

Some prefer placing their physical documents into a 3-ring binder, with dividers separating the categories. Clearly label the dividers, and if there are a lot of sections, it's a good idea to place a Table of Contents at the front of the binder to assist your survivors in finding the info they need without having to thumb through the whole binder.

You may prefer separating the documents by category into file folders in one location, such as an office tote, a file cabinet drawer, or a safe. Label the folders clearly, and provide a list of folders at the front of the File if you feel it will help your survivors.

DIGITAL DOCUMENTATION

Digital files (word-processing documents, spreadsheets, and PDFs) have advantages over physical files. One is that your survivors can make a digital copy available to an interested party by emailing it.

There's a good chance that some of the information you want to provide your survivors is already in digital form. You can print it out and include it in a physical file, or you can provide instructions on accessing it in its digital location, such as on a portable hard drive, a USB flash drive, an SD card, or in an encrypted online data storage service like Dropbox.

You can also convert documents that are currently in physical form into digital format. This is easily accomplished using one of the many mobile phone apps that take pictures of documents and turn them into PDFs. Search for "PDF Scanner" in the app store on your phone, and you will see a variety of such apps available.

For some, it may be appropriate to name a "digital executor" whose role is to manage all your digital assets on behalf of your survivors. If you decide to do that, you should make separate instructions for the digital executor. And, in your Survivor File, refer your survivors to the designated executor.

FILE LOCATION

The existence of a Survivor File is only meaningful if the appropriate people know of its existence and can locate it when needed. Once you have created your File and stored it securely, let those you predict will be your survivors know of its existence and its location. And be sure to inform them immediately if you move the File later.

Be specific about its location. For physical documentation, ensure the drawer, binder, or tote is marked "Survivor File" so that it is easily recognizable and does not blend into the scenery of the area.

SECURITY

Since your Survivor File will contain your most important and sensitive personal information, you must consider how it can be stored discreetly and securely, inaccessible to anyone but its intended audience.

Giving your survivors clear instructions about the security you've put in place is also essential. The File will only be helpful if your survivors can gain access to it.

HAVE A BACKUP

There are risks associated with having a single physical file, such as loss due to fire, water damage, etc. For this reason, many people decide to make an "emergency" copy of their File and store it in a different location than the first, possibly with one of the survivors, the family lawyer, or another representative.

FILE MAINTENANCE

Out-of-date information helps no one. Make a note in your calendar to update your File regularly. For instance, add a message on the last Saturday of every third month to review your File and update any recently changed information.

Also, make a mental note not to wait for your calendar prompt to update the File, but whenever possible, make the change to the File while it's still fresh in memory. This is especially important for specific information in your File, such as your instructions for the care and support of your dependents, which must always remain accurate and relevant.

5

IMPORTANT CONTACTS

Your survivors will benefit from having the contact information for all your important contacts in one place. Provide a list with names, emails, phone numbers, and addresses if appropriate.

- Financial adviser
- Lawyer
- Accountant
- Tax return preparer
- Insurance Broker
- Family members and friends who should be notified of your passing

6

FUNERAL AND BURIAL

If you leave specific instructions, your survivors will not have to play a guessing game regarding what you prefer regarding your funeral and burial. Their task will be complicated enough—there's no good reason to leave them the task of sorting this out as well.

The instructions you leave for your survivors are highly personal, and you can express your wishes in a way that reflects your beliefs and values. These instructions will outline how you want your funeral, memorial service, or burial to be conducted.

The first thing your survivors will want to know is if you have already made arrangements with a funeral home or cemetery and if you've chosen a specific religious institution to be involved.

- **Type of Funeral Service**: Specify whether you prefer a funeral service, memorial service, celebration of life, or another type of gathering.
- **Burial or cremation**: Specify your preference for either burial or cremation.
- **Location**: Specify your preferred locations for the service, the burial, the reception, and the disposition of your remains in the case of cremation.
- **Pre-arrangements**: Provide any agreements or contracts you have with a cemetery or funeral home and the contact information.
- **Church or religious institution**: Provide the contact information.
- **Service details**: Specify your preferred order of service, religious or cultural customs, rituals, readings, poems, music, or other personalized elements you would like to be included in the service.
- **Officiant or speaker**: Specify your preferred individual to officiate the service. If you have no individual in mind, state how you wish them to be chosen.
- **Donation to medical research**: Specify your wishes concerning donating your body or organs to medical research.
- **Memorial donations**: Specify the organization(s) you would like to receive

memorial donations in your name. Or, you can specify that individuals can donate to the organization of their choice.
- **Funeral reception**: Specify the location and type of activity you would like to follow the funeral—a reception, meal, or another gathering—and any specific food, beverages, or activities you would like to be involved.
- **Funeral expenses**: It will be very helpful for your survivors to know if you have designated specific funds or assets to cover the funeral expenses.
- **Obituary and funeral announcements**: Specify your preferences for the content and distribution of obituary notices or funeral announcements.

7

ADVANCE DIRECTIVES

Advance directives (Health Care and Medical Directives) are documents used to communicate one's healthcare preferences and wishes in advance, to be considered when the individual can't speak or decide for themselves.

Everyone should consider having a Living Will and a Power of Attorney in their Survivor File and on file with their primary care physician. To create these directives, you can consult an attorney or use the standardized forms provided by your local government or healthcare organizations. Letting your family know you have made Advance Directives is also a good idea.

- **Living Will**: Specify your preferences for end-of-life decisions, such as the use of life-sustaining treatments like feeding tubes, ventilators, and resuscitation, in the event you become incapacitated or unable to communicate your wishes.

- **Durable Power of Attorney for Healthcare** (or Health Care Proxy, or Medical Power of Attorney): You may already have a General Durable Power of Attorney document which designates a specific individual to make financial decisions for you if you can't speak or decide for yourself. Similarly, the Durable Power of Attorney for Healthcare is a legal form that lets you name the person you want to make treatment decisions for you if you can't speak or decide for yourself.

*I*t is also highly recommended that those with terminal illnesses consult with their healthcare providers about the possible need for either or both of the following two documents.

- **Do-Not-Resuscitate (DNR)**: A DNR, an advance directive that indicates a person's desire to forgo CPR in the event of cardiac or respiratory arrest, is generally used for individuals with terminal illnesses for whom

attempting resuscitation would be unlikely to result in an acceptable recovery.
- **Medical Orders for Life-Sustaining Treatment (MOLST)**: Like the DNR, this form is also used for people with terminal illnesses, but where the DNR is limited to instructions about the use of CPR, the MOLST form covers a variety of end-of-life treatments (such as intubation and artificial nutrition).

8

OFFICIAL DOCUMENTS

Official documents are those legal and government-issued documents that help to establish your identity, citizenship status, and other personal information. Your survivors will likely need soem or all of these documents, and you'll help them greatly by locating them in a single location within your Survivor File.

The more common items included in this category are listed below. Please note that the specific documents will vary depending on your country of residence, local regulations, and circumstances.

- Birth certificate
- Marriage license
- Divorce papers

- Birth certificate/adoption papers for minor children
- National ID card
- Social Security card
- Passport
- Citizenship or naturalization certificate
- Residency permit or Visa
- Drivers license
- Auto title
- Military record

You should also consider your legacy. For instance, you may expect to receive ongoing recognition for an achievement made in your field. In this case, it could be helpful for your survivors to have access to other documents such as:

- Academic degrees and transcripts
- Awards and other forms of recognition
- Contracts for your work
- Manuscripts, speeches, and presentations
- Copyrights and trademarks

9

CARE AND SUPPORT FOR DEPENDENTS

Dependents are those who depend on you for care and support, including:

- Minor children
- Elderly parents
- Persons with special needs
- Pets

Leaving instructions for their care and support is essential to ensure their well-being when you cannot assist.

To ensure the legal authority of the instructions you leave, it is a good idea to consult with an attorney to ensure you have the appropriate legal documents, such as a will, guardianship or conservatorship powers, and powers of attorney.

. . .

However you choose to leave instructions, you must consider which details from the list below are required for each dependent.

- Identification of the person with enough clarity and detail that there can be no question about who is being referred to
- Location and access information for the financial resources available for dependent care and support
- Living arrangements for those living in a residence other than your primary residence, including address, lease or ownership information, utility payments, and instructions for maintenance and repairs
- Living arrangements for those living in a caregiving facility, including care plan, payment details, contact information, and address of the facility
- Your selection of caregiver if you have a specific recommendation or preference for caregiver or guardian; or if not, outline the qualities you deem essential when selecting such an individual
- Individuals to be notified in emergencies

- Medical information including allergies, existing medical conditions, medications, contact information for their healthcare providers, ongoing medical treatments and therapies, and any other specific needs
- Daily care needs and routines, including dietary restrictions, preferred activities, and any necessary equipment or supplies they require
- Educational needs for school-age children, including which school they attend, contact information for their teachers and administrators, and information about any special activities or extracurriculars

ASSETS AND VALUABLES

The asset category includes any of your personal belongings which are valuable enough that you want to make your survivors aware of them. *Valuables*, a subset of assets, refers to assets with *substantial* financial or sentimental value.

This list will be critical if you have:

- Valuables that will need to be secured immediately by your survivors
- A valuable your survivors may only find if you inform them of its existence and location
- An asset your survivors would only recognize as valuable if you provide information about its valuation

Given that one part of the definition of a valuable is that its value may be sentimental, your choice of what to consider a "valuable" will involve a certain element of subjectivity. Items such as cash, gold, and diamonds will surely make the list, but others, such as a roll-top desk built by your grandfather, may or may not. Something like this may have no intrinsic value on the antique market, but it may be of great worth to you and your family.

Typical items found in lists of valuables are:

- Primary residence (mortgage docs, deed, etc.)
- Other real estate (mortgage docs, deed, etc.)
- Timeshare ownership (mortgage docs, deed, etc.)
- Notes held (loans by you to others)
- Cemetery deed
- Safe deposit box
- Vehicles
- Boats
- Machinery
- Investments – stocks
- Investments – bonds
- Investments – commodities

CREATING A SURVIVOR FILE

- Investments – real estate
- Investments – currencies
- Brokerage accounts
- Partnerships and corporate ownership
- Digital assets
- Intangible assets – Intellectual property (patents, trademarks, copyrights, brand names, software, licenses, etc.)
- Currency (domestic and foreign)
- Cryptocurrency (Bitcoin, etc.)
- Credit cards (both bank-issued and store-branded)
- Bonds
- Bills of exchange
- Bank, Treasury, or promissory notes
- Gold, silver, or other precious metals
- Gemstones
- Jewelry and watches
- Collectible coins and currency
- Collectible stamps
- Fine art
- Rare books
- Antiques and historical artifacts
- Audio systems
- Video equipment
- Musical instruments and equipment
- Cameras and photographic equipment
- Scientific equipment
- Sports and recreational equipment

- Computers, tablets, mobile phones
- Any other personal belongings of value

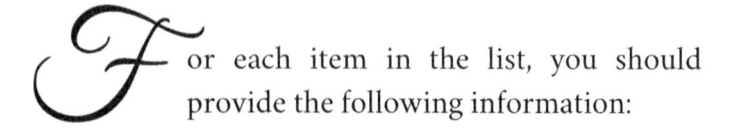

For each item in the list, you should provide the following information:

- Item
- Value
- Location
- Access
- Instructions about the distribution of the asset
- All relevant ownership documentation (For example, for your primary residence and other properties, provide the deeds, mortgages, closing and payoff documents, taxation valuation reports, and property surveys.)

NOTE: Designating who you want to receive an asset will not be necessary if you have a will in which you have already given legacy instructions. (A legacy is a specific bequest in a will, where the person making the will designates which assets are to be given to individuals or organizations.) Whether stated in your will or your Survivor File, it's crucial to identify the beneficiaries and ensure that the description of the asset is detailed enough to avoid ambiguity.

PHYSICAL ASSETS

Given the variety of possible assets, there is no one example that will satisfy all situations. As you make your list of assets, be sure to provide the six pieces of information mentioned earlier and add anything else you feel is important for your survivors to know.

In the following three examples, Jim and Jane have ensured their survivors can locate the asset, understand its value, and distribute the asset according to their wishes.

- **JIM'S GRANDAD'S ROLLTOP DESK**
- In unit 345 at Monroe Storage, 11 Monroe Street, phone number 234-777-9090
- The key to the unit is on both of our keyrings
- We would like Jennifer to have this

- **JIM'S GRANDAD'S RIFLE**
- Civil War - Enfield Pattern 53 Short Musket
- Above the mantle in the family room
- Similar rifles sold for $650-700 in online antique gun auction sites (2017)
- We would like Sam to have this

- **COIN COLLECTION**
- In three green binders in the safe in Jim's office.
- The combination of the safe is written on a piece of paper in the physical "Survivor File."
- Valued at $22,000 by C&S Antiques in Hamilton (2012).
- To be split evenly between Sam, Jennifer, and John.

ASSETS MANAGED VIA WEBSITE

For an asset that is accessed via a website (such as an IRA) you will need to provide your survivors the website address (URL) and its unique login credentials. Login credentials include anything the website asks you to provide when you attempt to sign into the website, including:

- Website address (URL)
- Username
- Password

- Account ID
- Personal identifiers (phone number, email address, etc.)
- Any other required codes
- Security questions and answers

You can make a table or spreadsheet listing your assets and the website information needed for each, or you can simply write it in list form, as shown in the example below.

- **HASBORG INVESTMENTS (IRAs)**
- https://www.hasborg.com
- Username: JJfamily43
- Password: tyu-34GtY-ste
- Code: The website will send a 4-digit code to Jim's phone
- Jim's IRA Account ID: 36476-25
- Jane's Account ID: 65492-63

Alternatively, if you have a password management app in which you have stored all of your login credentials, your entry could look something like the following example, in which the second bullet has replaced three of the bullets in the above example.

- **HASBORG INVESTMENTS (IRAs)**
- https://www.hasborg.com

- See the "Password Safe" app on both of our phones for our logon credentials. (The password for the app is written on a piece of paper in our Survival File.)
- Jim's IRA Account ID: 36476-25
- Jane's Account ID: 65492-63

A BETTER WAY (RECOMMENDED!)

The most efficient way to provide this information is to direct your survivors to the information stored on your computer. It is not only a more elegant solution for them, it also will help you get and stay organized yourself! Here's how it works…

Make use of the *Favorites* (or *Bookmarks*) in the browser window of your computer. These are "links" to the websites you use (you click on one, and your computer navigates to that website immediately).

First, you will create a list of links for the websites of your asset accounts. Then, in your Survivor File, you can simply direct your survivors to it.

For example, on the "Assets" page in Jim and Jane's Survivor File, they provide these instructions:

- *Links to our Asset websites can be found on Jim's laptop, in the "Safari" web browser, in the drop-down of the "Assets" tab.*
- *The logon credentials for each of these accounts can be found in the "Password Safe" app on both of our laptops and on both of our phones. (The app's password is written on a piece of paper in our Survival File.)*

Accompanying the instructions, they provide this screenshot from their computer

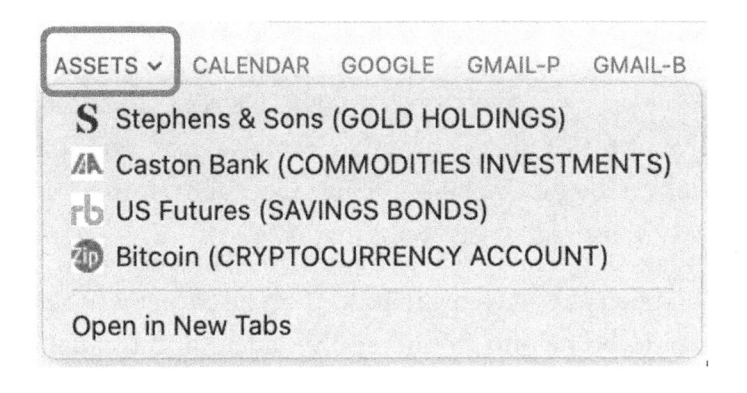

```
ASSETS ⌄  | CALENDAR   GOOGLE   GMAIL-P   GMAIL-B
S  Stephens & Sons (GOLD HOLDINGS)
A  Caston Bank (COMMODITIES INVESTMENTS)
rb US Futures (SAVINGS BONDS)
🅱 Bitcoin (CRYPTOCURRENCY ACCOUNT)

Open in New Tabs
```

As you can see, Jim and Jane have:

1. A list of accounts in the form of a list of website links on Jim's computer, and
2. A list of login credentials contained in a password management app that they've loaded on their phones and computers

By simply pasting a screenshot of the list of website links and adding a few instructions, they have been able to provide their survivors with directions to:

- A list of assets
- Links to the websites of these assets
- Directions to the login credentials for these websites

Some things to note about this example:

1. Jim and Jane use Safari as their web browser, so they saved their website links as "Favorites." Other web browsers also save website links. Google Chrome, for instance, allows users to save website links as "Bookmarks."

2. When they saved the links, they used names that would be helpful to and easily understood by their survivors.

3. Jim and Jane installed a password management app on their phones and computers in which they can save all their login credentials. Many of these apps are available; if you are not currently using one, this may be the time to start.

4. There is a "master password" to open the password management app, which they have made avail-

able to their survivors on a sheet of paper in their Survivors File.

ASSETS WITH NO ONLINE PRESENCE

It's also possible that you have an asset that does not fit the "physical" or the "website-based" categories. It may be an asset in the form of a contract or agreement with an individual or company that does not offer a way to manage your business with them online.

In these cases, you must provide your survivors with a detailed description of the asset and the contact information for those they'll need to work with to manage it.

As before, you can make a table or spreadsheet listing these assets or simply write the list in paragraph form. For example, on the "Assets" page in Jim and Jane's Survivor File, they provided this asset description:

- ***REAL ESTATE INVESTMENTS W/ WYTHCOMB INC.***
  - *We have two contracts ("Joint Development Agreements") with Wythcomb, Inc.*
  - *The contact information for Wythcomb, Inc. and all the documentation for these investments is located in the red binder*

labeled *"Real Estate Investments" in the filing cabinet*
- *NOTE: These are 5-year contracts, both coming due on April 12, 2023, at which time we will receive our equity and profit.*

*A*lternatively, if the documentation is in digital form, you can simply provide instructions on where to find the information. For example, on the "Assets" page in Jim and Jane's Survivor File, they provided this screenshot from their computer:

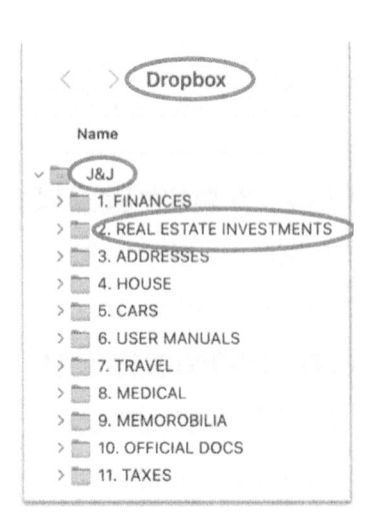

```
<  >  (Dropbox)

Name
v  (J&J)
  >  1. FINANCES
  >  2. REAL ESTATE INVESTMENTS
  >  3. ADDRESSES
  >  4. HOUSE
  >  5. CARS
  >  6. USER MANUALS
  >  7. TRAVEL
  >  8. MEDICAL
  >  9. MEMOROBILIA
  >  10. OFFICIAL DOCS
  >  11. TAXES
```

Accompanying the screenshot, they included these instructions:

- ***REAL ESTATE INVESTMENTS W/ WYTHCOMB INC.***
- *We have two contracts ("Joint Development Agreements") with Wythcomb, Inc.*
- *In the "Dropbox" folder on the desktop of both of our laptops, in the "J&J" folder, there is a "Real Estate Investments" folder.*
- *The contact information for Wythcomb, Inc. and all the documentation for these investments is located in the folder*

11

INCOME SOURCES

It is also crucial to ensure that your survivors know of all expected future income, whether you receive it periodically or expect a one-time payment. Money that is due to you runs the risk of going unclaimed if your survivors are not aware of the specific financial obligation to you. Unfortunately, many millions of dollars a year are never transferred to the rightful heirs because of a lack of planning and communication.

Providing your survivors with a list of income sources will help ensure that is not the case for your family. It will also give them the information they need to make sense of this side of your financial picture. It can get confusing if they don't know why checks are arriving, or funds are automatically deposited in your bank account.

Some common income sources are:

- Employer
- Social Security
- Pension
- Annuities
- IRA distributions
- Gifts received (taxable)
- Alimony
- Rents (paid to you)
- Payments (to you, on loans made by you)
- Time deposits
- Interest and dividends

NOTE: You may already have provided the necessary information for some of these items in your list of assets.

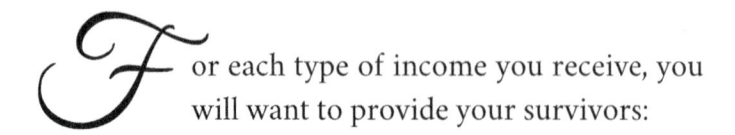

For each type of income you receive, you will want to provide your survivors:

- The source
- The source's contact information
- The dollar amount
- The frequency
- How the income payments are received
- Any other details needed by them to access and manage the obligation

For example, on the Income page in Jim and Jane's Survivor File, they provided the following list of five income sources:

- COSTCO (Jim's employer))
- Sam Johnson, Supervisor, 657-098-0234
- Paycheck auto-deposited into our Bank of America checking account every second Thursday

- DEWEY PATRIES AND PIES (Jane's employer)
- 1423 Main Street in Dewey
- Sarah Johnson, Manager, 657-909-8976
- Paycheck auto-deposited into our Bank of America checking account on the 1st and 15th

- JIM'S DELAWARE STATE RETIREMENT
- **This is also payable to Jane for life**
- Delaware State Pension Agency / 800-444-2736
- https://www.delpension.gov (See the "Password Safe" app for our logon credentials)
- $1850 per month auto-deposited into our Bank of America checking account

- RENTS FROM PROPERTIES WE OWN IN PARTNERSHIP WITH SMYTH & LYON
- Smyth & Lyon, LLC / 333-909-2346
- The loan documents are in the file folder "Properties" in the filing cabinet
- Smyth & Lyon send a check for $1975 every June, September, December, and March

- LOAN TO BOB FRANKLIN
- This was startup capital for his printing company
- Bob's phone: 560-765-0980
- The loan documents are in the file folder "Franklin Loan" in the filing cabinet
- Bob sends a $975 check by mail to the house at the beginning of every month
- The last payment will be July 2027

12

ACCOUNTS

Your survivors will need a list of the companies with which you do business and to whom you make payments, which we will call "accounts." Some of the most common are listed below.

- Rent or leases paid by you
- Credit Accounts – Visa, American Express, etc.
- Credit Accounts – stores, online retailers, etc.
- Memberships and subscriptions
- Online cash sending/receiving services – PayPal, Venmo, Wise, Etc.
- Home utilities – electric, gas, trash, cable, internet, phone
- Maintenance contracts (lawn service, pool service, AC service, etc.)

- Highway toll systems (you may have a balance owed or due)
- Online retailers (with whom you have established an "account" to submit an order—Amazon, Zappos Shoes, etc.
- Amazon paid subscriptions (Amazon Music, TV channels, etc.)
- Apple paid subscriptions (iCloud, Apple Music, etc.)
- Entertainment (Netflix, YouTube, Hulu, Paramount+, Disney, etc.)
- Online buying & selling (Craigslist, eBay, etc.)
- Prescription delivery services (OptumRX, GoodRX, CVS, etc.)
- Travel services (Airbnb, VRBO, Expedia, Renta-Car, Uber, Lyft, etc.)
- Convenience services (Grubhub, Instacart, etc.)
- Online services with a monthly or yearly fee (Microsoft Office 365, etc.)
- Online memberships (Paid Instructional Sites, etc.)
- Club memberships (AARP, AAA, etc.)
- Subscriptions to newspapers, magazines, wine clubs, etc.)

NOTE: **Funeral home contracts** are dealt with in Chapter 6, **cemetery deeds** in Chapter 10, **mort-**

gages in Chapter 10, **income sources** in Chapter 11, **bank accounts** in Chapter 14, and **insurance policies** in Chapters 17-19.

*Y*our survivors will be able to access and manage most, if not all, of your accounts online. Create either a list, a table, or a spreadsheet that provides the website address (URL) and the logon credentials for each service, using the methods described in the section, *Assets Managed Via Websites*, in Chapter 10.

Or, as shown in the section, *A Better Way,* in Chapter 10, you can create a list of website links and then direct your survivors to it. For example, on the "Accounts" page in Jim and Jane's Survivor File, they provided the following screenshot from their computer.

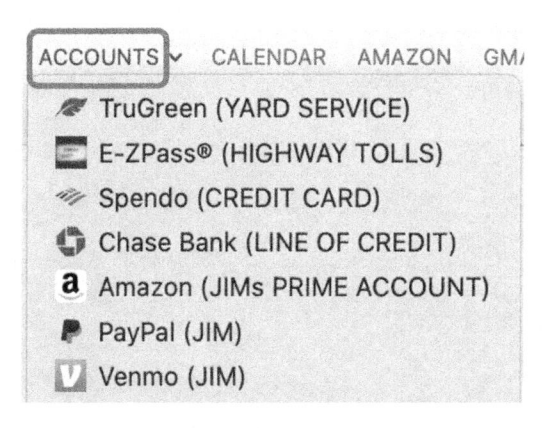

ACCOUNTS   CALENDAR   AMAZON   GM/
- TruGreen (YARD SERVICE)
- E-ZPass® (HIGHWAY TOLLS)
- Spendo (CREDIT CARD)
- Chase Bank (LINE OF CREDIT)
- Amazon (JIMs PRIME ACCOUNT)
- PayPal (JIM)
- Venmo (JIM)

Accompanying the screenshot, they provided these instructions:

- *Links to our Accounts websites can be found on Jim's laptop, in the "Safari" web browser, in the drop-down of the "Accounts" tab.*
- *The logon credentials for each of these accounts can be found in the "Password Safe" app on both of our laptops and on both of our phones. (The app's password is written on a piece of paper in our Survival File.)*

13

SERVICES

The category "Services" is very similar to the accounts category. You have entered into a relationship by providing the company with your personal information. Still, we're not considering it an account because you never, or very infrequently, make a payment to them.

Since these companies have your personal information, it is vital that your survivors know of these relationships. In some instances, they may deem it necessary to ensure the account is closed.

Given the vast number of services that do business online, the list of possibilities for this category is endless. The suggestions below will help you as you build your list.

- Social networking (Facebook, Pinterest, etc.)

- Digital storage (Dropbox, Google, etc.)
- Video conferencing (Skype, Zoom, etc.)
- Real estate sites (Realtor, Trulia, Zillow, etc.)
- Tax preparation (TurboTax, etc.)
- Foundations (cancer research, etc.)
- Personal website
- Pet microchip service
- Digital greeting card service
- Online magazine subscriptions
- Airline loyalty programs
- Hotel loyalty programs
- Public library

Create either a list, a table, or a spreadsheet that provides the website address (URL) and the logon credentials for each service, using the methods described in the section, *Assets Managed Via Websites*, in Chapter 10.

Or, as shown in the section, *A Better Way*, in Chapter 10, you can create a list of website links and then direct your survivors to it. For example, on the "Services" page in Jim and Jane's Survivor File, they provided the following screenshot from their computer:

CREATING A SURVIVOR FILE

> **SERVICES** ✓   CALENDAR   AMAZON   GM.
> - 🅢 Skype (JIM ACCOUNT)
> - 📦 Dropbox (JANE ACCOUNT)
> - ✅ TurboTax® (BOTH)
> - 🌹 American Greetings (ECARDS)
> - 🐾 Petfinder (FIDO'S MICROCHIP)
> - 🏨 Hilton Honors (JIM)

Accompanying the screenshot, they provided these instructions:

- *Links to our Services websites can be found on Jim's laptop, in the "Safari" web browser, in the drop-down of the "Services" tab.*
- *The logon credentials for each of these accounts can be found in the "Password Safe" app on both of our laptops and on both of our phones. (The app's password is written on a piece of paper in our Survival File.)*

14

BANK ACCOUNTS

Knowing where you keep your cash assets is very important for survivors. Federal laws require unclaimed deposit accounts to be transferred to the state after 18 months. Providing a list of bank accounts is one way to avoid having your assets lost to your family and becoming property of the state.

To assist you in developing a comprehensive list of all your banking relationships, the most common types of banks and accounts are listed below.

Types of banks:

- Retail (personal and small business banking)
- Credit Union (personal banking)
- Savings and Loan Associations / Thrift banks (mortgages)

- Challenger banks and Neo-banks (Non-traditional online banks)
- Commercial (small-to-medium business)
- Investment (large business; large personal portfolio)

Types of bank accounts:

- Checking
- Savings
- Money Market
- Certificate of Deposit
- Mortgage
- Line of credit

NOTE: **Credit cards** are not included here because they are dealt with in Chapter 12, and **safe deposit boxes** in Chapter 10.

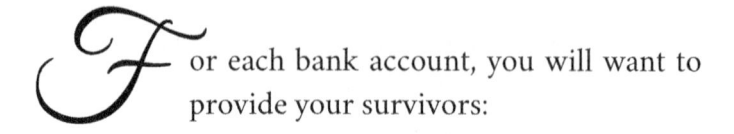

For each bank account, you will want to provide your survivors:

- The name of the bank
- The type of account
- Your account number
- Contact information for the bank
- Website

- Login credentials for the website
- The location of account documentation (checkbook, loan agreement, etc.)
- Other pertinent details (such as the name of the account owner)

15

MEDICAL PROVIDERS AND MEDICAL HISTORY

Survivors frequently settle accounts with medical providers, including:

- Dentists
- Optometrists
- Primary care physicians
- Dermatologists
- Cardiologists
- Other specialists
- Veterinarians (if pets are involved)

For each, provide your survivors with the necessary contact information:

- Physician's name
- Name of the clinic or practice
- Address

- Phone number
- Website or patient portal
- Login credentials for the website

Again, you can create a list, a table, or a spreadsheet that lists your medical providers.

Or, as shown in the section, *A Better Way,* in Chapter 10, you can create a list of website links and then direct your survivors to it. For example, on the "Medical Providers" page in Jim and Jane's Survivor File, they included the following screenshot from their computer.

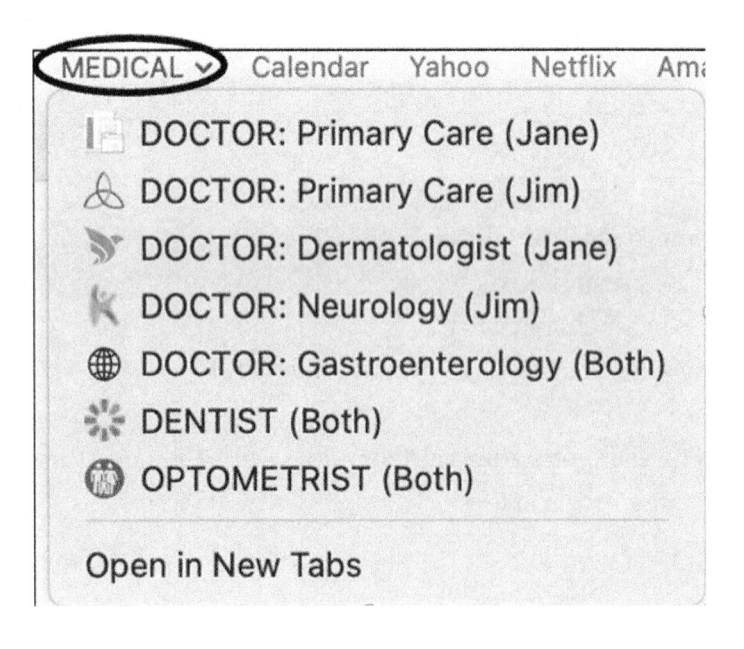

(MEDICAL ⌄) Calendar   Yahoo   Netflix   Am

- DOCTOR: Primary Care (Jane)
- DOCTOR: Primary Care (Jim)
- DOCTOR: Dermatologist (Jane)
- DOCTOR: Neurology (Jim)
- DOCTOR: Gastroenterology (Both)
- DENTIST (Both)
- OPTOMETRIST (Both)

Open in New Tabs

Accompanying the screenshot, they included these instructions:

- *Links to the websites of all of our medical providers can be found on Jim's laptop, in the "Safari" web browser, in the drop-down of the "Medical" tab.*
- *The logon credentials for each of these websites (patient portals) can be found in the "Password Safe" app on both of our laptops and on both of our phones. (The app's password is written on a piece of paper in our Survival File.)*

MEDICAL HISTORY

In some cases, it will also be very helpful to your survivors to have particular aspects of your medical history, to help them understand your relationship with the provider. For example, seeing a gastroenterologist regularly every three months for a chronic condition is much different than seeing one every five years as part of a wellness program.

16

HEALTH INSURANCE

This category includes health insurance (individual or family), prescription insurance, vision insurance, dental insurance, and any other insurance which covers some aspect of your physical or mental health.

When listing these accounts, be sure also to include billing and payment details (as in the Billing row in the example below) so that your survivors are made aware of these financial obligations and can manage them appropriately.

- Insurance company
- Name of the insurance plan
- Your member ID (if applicable)
- Your group number (if applicable)

- Your account number (if applicable)
- Insurance broker contact information
- Website address and logon credentials
- Billing and payment details
- Other pertinent details

For example, on the *Health Insurance* page in Jim and Jane's Survivor File, they provided the following information:

- UNITED HEALTHCARE / MEDICARE ADVANTAGE
- https://www.uhealth.org
- See the "Password Safe" app on both of our phones for our login credentials. (The password for the app is written on a piece of paper in our Survival File.)
- Member ID: 365479850
- The premium is paid monthly by auto-withdrawal from our Bank of America checking account.

NOTE: As with many of the previous categories, you may want to provide information about your insurance providers by creating a list of website links in an "Insurance" tab in your web browser (as shown in the section, *A Better Way* in Chapter 10.) You could include links to your Health Insurance provider, your Life Insurance provider (Chapter 17), your Long Term Care Insurance provider (Chapter 18), and any other insurance providers (Chapter 19).

LIFE INSURANCE

Life insurance policies are of particular importance to survivors for obvious reasons, and it is incumbent upon you to provide all the information necessary for your survivors to submit their claims.

Over the past twenty years, life insurers have paid out $1.1 trillion to the beneficiaries of life insurance policies. But unfortunately, many millions of dollars have gone unclaimed during that same time simply because the beneficiaries were unaware the policies existed.

Be sure to include this information and anything else you feel your survivors need to know:

- The name of the insurer
- The date the policy expires

- The value of the policy
- The policy number
- Instructions on how/where to view the policy documents
- Instructions on how/where to view the beneficiary nomination forms
- How the premiums are paid
- The contact information necessary to file a claim

Some people may also stipulate what they expect their survivors to use the policy proceeds for. For instance, it may be that you do not have any money set aside expressly for your funeral expenses, and you want the proceeds to cover those expenses.

18

LONG TERM CARE INSURANCE

When other family members are called upon to make medical and financial decisions for you or your surviving spouse, they must have information about your LTC Insurance, if you have it.

Most importantly, be sure to provide them with these details:

- The name of the insurer
- The policy number
- Your agent's contact information
- Any other contact information necessary to file a claim
- How the premiums are currently being paid
- The total value of the policy
- The daily allowance

- Instructions on how/where to view the policy documents
- Any other details you feel your survivors should know upfront, without having to read all the policy documents

For example, on the *Long Term Care Insurance* page in Jim and Jane's Survivor File, they provided the following information:

- **NEW YORK LIFE INSURANCE CO.**
- Agent: John Vincent, 573-098-4638
- Jim's Policy Number: 968700
- Jane's Policy Number: 767858
- Premiums are paid monthly by auto-withdrawal from our Bank of America checking account
- The policy documents are in the file folder "LTC Insurance" in the filing cabinet
- NOTE: Each of us have $165,000 to use, at $150 per day, and payments can be made to a care facility, an in-home caregiver, or to a family member who is the care-giver

19

OTHER INSURANCE

This category is a catch-all for any other type of insurance you may have, such as:

- Employer death benefits
- Umbrella
- Auto
- Home
- Renter
- ID theft

As with the information provided about your other insurers, your survivors will need to know the following:

- The type of insurance
- The name of the insurer
- The date the policy expires

- The value of the policy
- The policy number
- Instructions on how/where to view the policy documents (online, physical documents, etc.)
- How the premiums are paid
- The contact information necessary to file a claim

20

CHARITABLE DONATIONS AND PHILANTHROPY

Many people, wanting to continue supporting causes they care about after their passing, address charitable bequests in their will. In that case, it is not necessary to duplicate those instructions in your File. But, given that 60% of American adults do not have a will or estate plan, it is more likely that your Survivors File will be the only place your survivors are provided this information.

A bequest designates a specific amount of money or property to be donated to a particular organization, whether a specific charity, foundation, educational institution, religious organization, or any other qualifying nonprofit entity.

For each organization you identify, you may also want to name an alternative beneficiary in case the intended charitable organization no longer exists when your survivors are carrying out your wishes.

Clarity and specificity are essential here. To ensure your wishes are accurately carried out, for each organization to which you want to donate, be sure to provide the following:

- The full legal name
- The full address
- Phone number
- Other contact information
- Website
- Website login credentials (if you have established an account with them which you use to make donations)
- Any other information you feel would be helpful in identifying and contacting the specific organization

In some jurisdictions, there are laws and regulations about donations such as these, so it is a good idea to do your research in advance to ensure that what you are asking your survivors to do is consistent with these. And, of course, there will be implications for your final tax return, so you should consult with your tax preparer also.

21

SMALL BUSINESSES

This category applies to you if you are one of the 30 million people in the United States who own a small business, and is especially important if you're one of the 27 million who own a business with no employees.

The most pressing question will be, should the business continue to operate or should it be closed? The answer to that question will determine how your survivors will use the rest of the information.

Whether they are closing the business or taking over management of it, they will need access to all of your business records. You may not be able to, or may not want to, physically include it in the Survivor File, but it is essential that you tell them how they can locate and access it.

If you have a large volume of business records, be sure to separate out and call attention to the following key types of information so that your survivors can easily find them.

- A signed statement stating how you want the business to be dealt with when you're gone
- Contact information for professional services used by the business (tax preparer, lawyer, insurance broker, etc.)
- Resource inventory: Equipment, supplies, technology systems, facilities, etc.
- Product inventory
- Suppliers and vendors
- Clients and customers
- Contracts
- Bookkeeping records (invoices, receipts, etc.)
- Filings with the state corporation commission
- Other official correspondence which explains important aspects of your company's official, legal, or tax status
- Employer Identification Number (EIN) from the IRS
- Corporate tax records for the last seven years
- Business-specific regulatory and legal compliance considerations

- Any other business-specific information necessary for daily operations

22

PERSONAL MESSAGES

While creating your Survivor File, you may decide to include special communications for your survivors in the form of:

- Personal messages
- Words of wisdom
- Life lessons
- A sense of one's life story
- Expressions of love and appreciation
- Shared memories
- Guidance for the future

These messages can be directed towards specific individuals or to all your survivors as a group. They can be handwritten, word-processed, video-recorded, or audio-recorded. Whatever the format, the primary purpose is to provide support and encouragement during a challenging time.

23

SHOW HOW MUCH YOU CARE EVEN AFTER YOU'RE GONE

For some of you, the thought of pulling together the information you need for your Survivor File is not a pleasant one. You may not be sure where to find some of the information. And the information you can locate is not well-organized. Just the thought of trying to remember all the online accounts you've opened in the last few years has you seriously considering throwing this book into the trash and forgetting you ever heard of it.

Before you do, STOP, and think about it. First, it's your decision about what to include. If certain information doesn't seem important enough to warrant the time and energy, skip it for now. Nothing says you couldn't go back later and include it. In the same way, there's no law of the universe demanding that you have your File completed in the next few weeks.

All that is required is that you START. Start at the beginning and take one step at a time. Consider this: if you work on one category weekly, you'll have your File completed in a few months!

Set some achievable goals, make a plan, and get started. It won't be nearly as difficult as you think. If you get stuck along the way and need some support and encouragement, contact me on my website (www.chrismeisinger.com), and I'll do my best to help you finish strong.

Benjamin Franklin said, "By failing to prepare, you are preparing to fail," and in this case, your loved ones will bear the cost of your failure. The key is to **remember how much of a favor you are doing for those you care about.**

ADDITIONAL RESOURCES

Creating a Survivor File was written with a specific audience in mind. People who:

- Have a good grasp of their own personal affairs.
- Know where to find the information they need when it comes to managing their affairs, financial and otherwise.
- Are very organized, somewhat organized, or not-at-all organized, but either way, they're

committed to making life easier for their survivors.
- Don't need or want a wealth of information—they want a simple easy-to-follow plan and a model that will help them clearly communicate the necessary essential information to their survivors.

The strength of *Creating a Survivor File* is that it offers a very **simple plan** that practically anyone can follow and promises results that will satisfy the needs of almost anyone finding themselves filling the role of "survivor."

But, for those of you whose personal estate is more complicated or nuanced than the average, or for those who just find your curiosity piqued and want to dive much deeper into the waters of end-of-life planning, take heart—there are excellent resources out there for you! Two of them in particular deserve your consideration:

Get It Together: Organize Your Records So Your Family Won't Have To. (Authors: Melanie Cullen and Shae Irving. Publisher: Nolo. The 10th edition was published in 2022.)

In Case You Get Hit By a Bus: How to Organize Your Life Now for When You're Not Around Later.

(Authors: Abby Schneiderman and Adam Seifer. Publisher: Workman Publishing. The 1st edition was published in 2020.)

Both of these books are a wealth of information about all things related to end-of-life planning. If that's what you're looking for, neither will disappoint.

* * *

And if I may, I'd like to ask a favor of you. If this book has been helpful, please take a few minutes to go online and leave a review. Your review really does matter. Providing honest feedback about how it helped you will assist others in their book-buying decisions. Thank you!

Printed in Great Britain
by Amazon